Essential Question:

Questions:	Notes:

Summary:

Essential Question:

Questions:	Notes:

Summary:

Essential Question:	
Questions:	**Notes:**

Summary:

Essential Question:

Questions:	Notes:

Summary:

Essential Question:

Questions:	Notes:

Summary:

Essential Question:

Questions:	Notes:

Summary:

Essential Question:

Questions:	**Notes:**

Summary:

Essential Question:

Questions:	Notes:

Summary:

Essential Question:

Questions:	**Notes:**

Summary:

Essential Question:

Questions:	Notes:

Summary:

Essential Question:

Questions:	Notes:

Summary:

Essential Question:

Questions:	**Notes:**

Summary:

Essential Question:	

Questions:	Notes:

Summary:

Essential Question:

Questions:	Notes:

Summary:

Essential Question:

Questions:	Notes:

Summary:

Essential Question:

Questions:	Notes:

Summary:

Essential Question:

Questions:	Notes:

Summary:

Essential Question:	
Questions:	**Notes:**
Summary:	

Essential Question:

Questions:	Notes:

Summary:

Essential Question:

Questions:	**Notes:**

Summary:

Essential Question:

Questions:	Notes:

Summary:

Essential Question:

Questions:	Notes:

Summary:

Essential Question:	
Questions:	**Notes:**
Summary:	

Essential Question:

Questions:	Notes:

Summary:

Essential Question:

Questions:	Notes:

Summary:

Essential Question:

Questions:	Notes:

Summary:

Essential Question:

Questions:	Notes:

Summary:

Essential Question:

Questions:	**Notes:**

Summary:

Essential Question:

Questions:	**Notes:**

Summary:

Essential Question:

Questions:	Notes:

Summary:

Essential Question:

Questions:	Notes:

Summary:

Essential Question:

Questions:	Notes:

Summary:

Essential Question:	
Questions:	**Notes:**
Summary:	

Essential Question:

Questions:	Notes:

Summary:

Essential Question:

Questions:	**Notes:**

Summary:

Essential Question:

Questions:	**Notes:**

Summary:

Essential Question:

Questions:	Notes:

Summary:

Essential Question:

Questions:	**Notes:**

Summary:

Essential Question:

Questions:	Notes:

Summary:

Essential Question:

Questions:	**Notes:**

Summary:

Essential Question:	
Questions:	**Notes:**
Summary:	

Essential Question:

Questions:	Notes:

Summary:

Essential Question:

Questions:	Notes:

Summary:

Essential Question:

Questions:	**Notes:**

Summary:

Essential Question:

Questions:	Notes:

Summary:

Essential Question:

Questions:	Notes:

Summary:

Essential Question:

Questions:	Notes:

Summary:

Essential Question:

Questions:	Notes:

Summary:

Essential Question:

Questions:	Notes:

Summary:

Essential Question:

Questions:	Notes:

Summary:

Essential Question:

Questions:	**Notes:**

Summary:

Essential Question:

Questions:	Notes:

Summary:

Essential Question:

Questions: | **Notes:**

Summary:

Essential Question:

Questions:	Notes:

Summary:

Essential Question:

Questions:	Notes:

Summary:

Essential Question:

Questions:	Notes:

Summary:

Essential Question:

Questions:	Notes:

Summary:

Essential Question:

Questions:	**Notes:**

Summary:

Essential Question:

Questions:	Notes:

Summary:

Essential Question:

Questions:	Notes:

Summary:

Essential Question:

Questions:	Notes:

Summary:

Essential Question:

Questions:	Notes:

Summary:

Essential Question:

Questions:	Notes:

Summary:

Essential Question:

Questions:	Notes:

Summary:

Essential Question:

Questions:	Notes:

Summary:

Essential Question:

Questions:	Notes:

Summary:

Essential Question:

Questions:	**Notes:**

Summary:

Essential Question:

Questions:	Notes:

Summary:

Essential Question:

Questions:	Notes:

Summary:

Essential Question:

Questions:	Notes:

Summary:

Essential Question:

Questions:	Notes:

Summary:

Essential Question:

Questions:	**Notes:**

Summary:

Essential Question:

Questions:	**Notes:**

Summary:

Essential Question:

Questions:	Notes:

Summary:

Essential Question:

Questions:	Notes:

Summary:

Essential Question:

Questions:	Notes:

Summary:

Essential Question:

Questions:	Notes:

Summary:

Essential Question:

Questions:	Notes:

Summary:

Essential Question:

Questions:	**Notes:**

Summary:

Essential Question:

Questions:

Notes:

Summary:

Essential Question:

Questions:	Notes:

Summary:

Essential Question:

Questions:	Notes:

Summary:

Essential Question:

Questions:	**Notes:**

Summary:

Essential Question:

Questions:	Notes:

Summary:

Essential Question:

Questions:	Notes:

Summary:

Essential Question:	
Questions:	Notes:
Summary:	

Essential Question:

Questions:	**Notes:**

Summary:

Essential Question:

Questions:	**Notes:**

Summary:

Essential Question:

Questions:	**Notes:**

Summary:

Essential Question:

Questions:	Notes:

Summary:

Essential Question:

Questions:	**Notes:**

Summary:

Essential Question:

Questions:	Notes:

Summary:

Essential Question:

Questions:	Notes:

Summary:

Essential Question:

Questions:	Notes:

Summary:

Essential Question:

Questions:	Notes:

Summary:

Essential Question:

Questions:	Notes:

Summary:

Essential Question:

Questions:	Notes:

Summary:

Essential Question:

Questions:	Notes:

Summary:

Essential Question:	
Questions:	**Notes:**
Summary:	

Essential Question:

Questions:	**Notes:**

Summary:

Essential Question:

Questions:	Notes:

Summary:

Essential Question:

Questions:	Notes:

Summary:

Essential Question:

Questions:	**Notes:**

Summary:

Essential Question:

Questions:	Notes:

Summary:

Essential Question:

Questions:	**Notes:**

Summary:

Essential Question:

Questions:	Notes:

Summary:

Essential Question:

Questions:	Notes:

Summary:

Essential Question:

Questions:	Notes:

Summary:

Essential Question:

Questions:	Notes:

Summary:

Essential Question:

Questions:	Notes:

Summary:

Made in the USA
Middletown, DE
22 September 2020

20316106R00062